SCIENCE
BUDDIES.

30-MINUTE
EDIBLE
SCIENCE
PROJECTS

Anna Leigh

Lerner Publications ➡ Minneapolis

Official Licensed Product
Lerner Publications Company
A division of Lerner Publishing Group, Inc.
241 First Avenue North
Minneapolis, MN 55401 USA

For reading levels and more information, look up this title at www.lernerbooks.com.

Main body text set in Hoosker Don't.
Typeface provided by The Chank Company.

Library of Congress Cataloging-in-Publication Data

Names: Leigh, Anna, author.
Title: 30-minute edible science projects / Anna Leigh.
Other titles: Thirty minute edible science projects
Description: Minneapolis : Lerner Publications, [2019] | Series: 30-minute makers |
    Audience: Ages 7–11. |
    Audience: Grades 4 to 6. | Includes bibliographical references and index.
Identifiers: LCCN 2018015746 (print) | LCCN 2018019037 (ebook) | ISBN
    9781541542891 (eb pdf) |
    ISBN 9781541538917 (lb : alk. paper)
Subjects: LCSH: Food—Experiments—Juvenile literature. | Science projects—Juvenile
    literature.
Classification: LCC TX355 (ebook) | LCC TX355 .L373 2019 (print) | DDC 507/.8—dc23

LC record available at https://lccn.loc.gov/2018015746

Manufactured in the United States of America
1-45074-35901-10/11/2018

CONTENTS

For even more edible
science projects,
scan this QR code!

FOOD SCIENCE

Did you know that the food you eat every day involves science? Using food, we can study physics, biology, and chemistry—and make some tasty treats while we're at it!

Many of the projects in this book involve heating and cooling food. When we change the temperature of food ingredients, we also change how they look and how their molecules behave. Molecules are always moving. When we cook, ingredients can change from solids (such as ice) to liquids (such as water) to gases (such as steam). The warmer an ingredient, the faster the molecules move and the more space between them. Changes in temperature create changes in ingredients and flavor. Let's get cooking!

BEFORE YOU GET STARTED

Many of these projects use common ingredients that you can find around your home, such as pots and pans, sugar, cups, and spoons. Other materials should be easy to find at a grocery store.

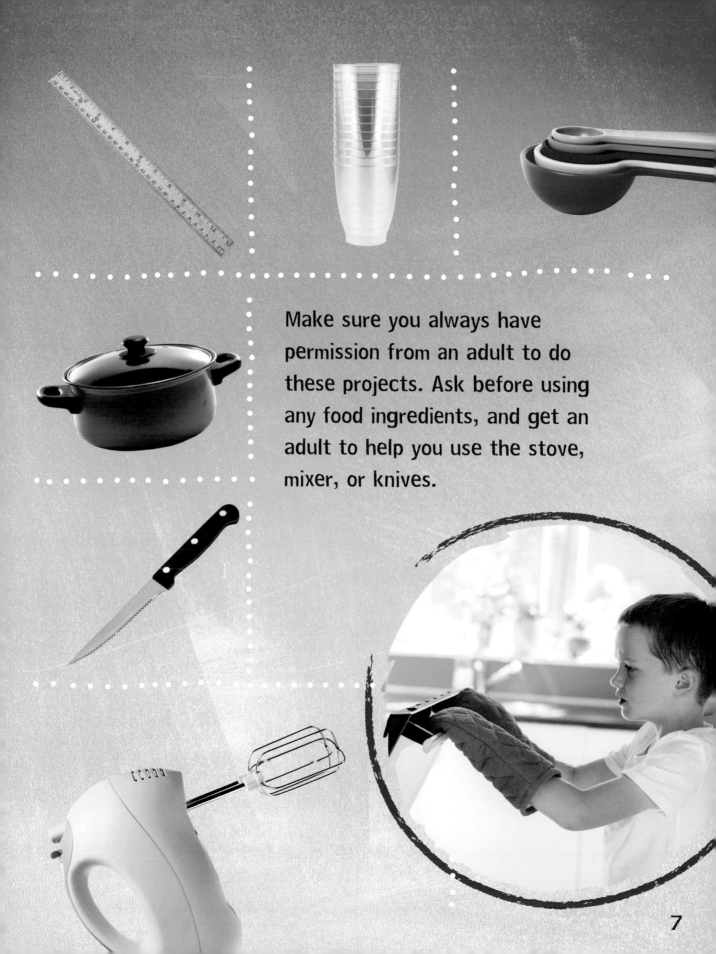

Make sure you always have permission from an adult to do these projects. Ask before using any food ingredients, and get an adult to help you use the stove, mixer, or knives.

CANDY SNAP

Did you know that sharing a piece of candy with a friend actually involves science?
Find out how different materials break and how temperature affects them.

🕐 **TIMEFRAME: 30 minutes**

MATERIALS

⇨ 2 each of a few different full-size candy bars

⇨ 2 each of a few different soft, gummy, or chewy candies that are long or big enough to hold with two hands

⇨ freezer

⇨ pencil and paper

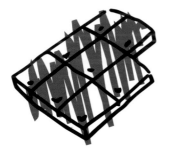

SCIENCE TAKEAWAY

Some materials are springy and flexible, and others are stiff and easy to break.
Most objects become less flexible when they are cold.

1. Place one of each type of candy in the freezer. Leave the other candies at room temperature.

2. Hold one of the room-temperature candies with one hand at either end.

3. Slowly bend the candy in half. How easy is it to bend?

4. Continue bending the candy until it breaks. Did it snap very suddenly or stretch out and break slowly? If the candy didn't break, can you break it by pulling it apart? Does it break suddenly or slowly?

5. Write down your observations about how each candy bent and broke.

6. Once frozen, remove the remaining candy from the freezer. Hold the candies with one hand at either end and repeat steps 3 to 5. Did the frozen candy bend and break differently?

HOMEMADE BUTTER

People once used a container called a butter churn to turn cream into butter. All you need is a jar and some super strong muscles!

🕐 **TIMEFRAME: 10-20 minutes**

MATERIALS

⇨ airtight jar

⇨ heavy cream at room temperature

SCIENCE TAKEAWAY

Cream is made up of water and globules of fat. When you shake cream, the fat globules clump together and separate from the water.

1 Pour the cream into the jar until the jar is about half full.

2 Screw the lid tightly onto the jar.

3 Hold the jar in your hand, and shake it hard for 5 to 20 minutes. You should start to see the cream changing within 10 minutes. Your butter is ready when it has completely separated from the liquid and forms a single, solid clump. The solid is butter, and the liquid is buttermilk.

DANCING CANDY HEARTS

Make candy hearts dance
in a glass of fizzy soda!

🕐 **TIMEFRAME: 15 minutes**

MATERIALS

⇨ 1 tall, clear glass

⇨ 1 unopened bottle
or can of clear soda

⇨ 4 conversation hearts

⇨ timer or stopwatch

⇨ pencil and paper

SCIENCE TAKEAWAY

Soda is full of carbon dioxide gas. Candy is heavier than soda, and gas is
lighter than soda. The heavy candy fell to the bottom of the glass, but then
bubbles of carbon dioxide attached to the candy and lifted it to the top.
At the top, the bubbles popped, and the candy fell back down.

1 Fill the glass nearly to the top with soda.

2 Drop the conversation hearts into the soda, one at a time. Start the timer or stopwatch. What happens to the candy hearts? Write down what you see.

3 Watch the glass for a few minutes. What happens to the candy hearts shortly after you drop them into the soda? How long did it take to change? Write down your observations.

4 Watch the glass for another 5 minutes. What happens to the candy hearts?

MAKE YOUR OWN SODA

You already know that soda is full of carbon dioxide, but how does the carbon dioxide gas get into the soda? Find out by making your very own fizzy soda!

🕐 **TIMEFRAME: 30 minutes**

MATERIALS

⇨ measuring spoons

⇨ citric acid

⇨ 5 plastic drinking cups

⇨ baking soda

⇨ measuring cups

⇨ water

⇨ spoon

⇨ sugar

⇨ food coloring

SCIENCE TAKEAWAY

When you combined the baking soda and citric acid, a chemical reaction happened to produce fizzy bubbles of carbon dioxide. The recipe with 1 teaspoon of baking soda probably made the most bubbles since there was more baking soda to react with the citric acid.

1 Add ¼ teaspoon of citric acid to three of your cups. Leave the other two cups empty.

2 Add ¹/₁₆ teaspoon of baking soda to one of the cups with citric acid.

3 Add ¼ cup of water to the cup with baking soda and citric acid. Stir the mixture with a spoon.

4 Add ¼ teaspoon of baking soda and ¼ cup of water to one of the other cups with citric acid. Mix the solution.

5 Add 1 teaspoon of baking soda and ¼ cup of water to the third cup with citric acid. Stir the mixture.

6 Taste the three solutions. How do they feel on your tongue?

7 Which mixture did you like best? Mix a new batch of it, using the same recipe as before. This time, add ¼ teaspoon of sugar. How does it taste?

8 Continue adding sugar, ¼ teaspoon at a time. Taste the mixture after each ¼ teaspoon, and keep track of how much you have added. When you've found a perfect soda recipe, add food coloring to make it look even more delicious. Then make more to share with your friends.

SWEET AND SOUR

What's your favorite food? Is it sweet, salty, bitter, sour, or savory? Do you know where these flavors come from? It has to do with chemistry.

⏱ **TIMEFRAME: 30 minutes**

MATERIALS

⇨ tape

⇨ marker

⇨ 3 glasses

⇨ measuring cup

⇨ water

⇨ measuring spoons

⇨ granulated sugar

⇨ mixing and tasting spoons

⇨ white wine vinegar

SCIENCE TAKEAWAY

Food has chemicals that interact with our taste buds to create tastes. Cooks combine chemicals to create balanced flavors. Small amounts of sour chemicals can balance larger amounts of sweet particles to create a pleasing flavor.

1. Use the tape and marker to label the glasses. Label the first glass "sugar water"; the second, "sugar and vinegar"; and the third, "vinegar water."

2. Measure 1 cup of water, and pour it into the sugar water glass.

3. Add 1 teaspoon of sugar to the glass of water. Stir until it has dissolved. Taste the sugar water. Is it sweet, pleasantly sweet, or too sweet?

4. Add 1 teaspoon of sugar, mix it, and taste it. Repeat this step three more times. When does the sugar water become pleasantly sweet? Did it become too sweet?

5. Pour half of the sugar water into the sugar and vinegar glass.

6. Add a quarter teaspoon of vinegar to the sugar and vinegar glass. Mix and taste the solution. How does it taste? Continue adding vinegar, a quarter teaspoon at a time, until the solution tastes pleasant. Write down how much vinegar you added.

7. Pour half a cup of water into the vinegar water glass. Then add the same amount of vinegar as you added to the sugar and vinegar glass. Mix and taste the solution. How does it taste?

TASTE TEST

Are some tastes easier to detect than others?
Find out just how sensitive your taste buds are.

🕐 **TIMEFRAME: 30 minutes**

MATERIALS

⇨ measuring spoons

⇨ distilled water

⇨ 12 paper or plastic cups

⇨ granulated sugar

⇨ spoons

⇨ marker and sticky notes

⇨ table salt

⇨ vinegar

⇨ paper towels

⇨ cotton swabs

SCIENCE TAKEAWAY

The taste buds on your tongue each have about 50 to 150 taste receptor cells. Taste molecules bind to these receptors and send a signal to your brain, so you can taste the flavor. Typically, salt and vinegar are easier to detect in small amounts than sugar is. Different people may taste things differently.

1 Pour 6 tablespoons of distilled water into a cup. Add 2½ teaspoons of sugar. Stir until it has dissolved. This gives you a 10 percent sugar solution.

2 Pour 2 teaspoons of the 10 percent sugar solution into a new cup. Add 6 tablespoons of water and stir. This gives you a 1 percent sugar solution.

3 Pour 2 teaspoons of the 1 percent sugar solution into a new cup. Add 6 tablespoons of water and stir. This gives you a 0.1 percent sugar solution.

4 Pour 2 teaspoons of the 0.1 percent sugar solution into a new cup. Add 6 tablespoons of water and stir. This gives you a 0.01 percent sugar solution. Label each cup with the correct percentage.

5 Repeat steps 1 to 4 to create salt solutions (starting with 1¾ teaspoons of salt) and vinegar solutions (starting with 2 teaspoons of vinegar).

6 Rinse your mouth with plain water. Wipe your tongue dry with a paper towel. Dip a clean cotton swab into the 10 percent sugar solution, and smear it on your tongue. Can you taste the sweetness?

7 Repeat step 6 with the other three sugar solutions. Rinse and wipe your mouth before each one. What is the lowest concentration in which you taste the sugar? Write this down.

8 Repeat steps 6 and 7 with the salt solutions and vinegar solutions.

MAKE ICE CREAM IN A BAG

Science is even involved in making ice cream! Learn how temperature changes ingredients, and make your own delicious treat.

🕐 **TIMEFRAME: 10–20 minutes**

MATERIALS

⇨ measuring spoons

⇨ sugar

⇨ measuring cup

⇨ half-and-half or heavy whipping cream

⇨ vanilla extract

⇨ 2 small plastic bags

⇨ 8 cups of ice cubes

⇨ 2 (1-gallon, or 3.8 L) plastic bags

⇨ salt

⇨ oven mitts

⇨ timer

SCIENCE TAKEAWAY

As ice melts, the temperature around it drops, so it refreezes before warming and melting more. Saltwater freezes at a lower temperature than pure water, so the bag with salt needs to get colder to refreeze. The colder temperature allows the ice cream ingredients to harden into ice cream.

1. Place 1 tablespoon of sugar, ½ cup of half-and-half, and ¼ teaspoon of vanilla into each small plastic bag. Seal the bags.

2. Add 4 cups of ice cubes to one of the gallon-sized bags. Add ½ cup of salt to the bag.

3. Place a small bag inside the large bag. Seal the large bag.

4. Put on oven mitts, and shake the bag for 5 minutes. Check every couple of minutes on the ingredients in the small bag. How cold does the bag feel?

5. Put 4 cups of ice into the other large bag. Do not add salt to this bag.

6. Place the other small bag inside the large bag. Seal the bag.

7. Repeat step 4 for this bag.

8. Did one of your bags make ice cream? Enjoy your tasty treat! (If one of the bags did not make ice cream, you can place it inside the bag of ice that worked and continue shaking.)

HOMEMADE MARSHMALLOWS

There's nothing else quite like marshmallows. They're squishy, spongy, chewy, and sweet. You can toast them over a fire and melt them in a mug of hot chocolate. What are they made of? Let's find out!

🕐 **TIMEFRAME**
PART 1: 30 minutes
PART 2: 20 minutes

MATERIALS

⇨ masking tape

⇨ pen or marker

⇨ 2 (8- or 9-inch, or 20 to 22 cm) foil cake or pie pans

⇨ vegetable oil

⇨ paper towels

⇨ powdered sugar

⇨ small strainer

⇨ measuring cups

⇨ water

⇨ large mixing bowl

⇨ 2 envelopes of plain, unflavored gelatin

⇨ fork

⇨ timer

⇨ granulated sugar

⇨ corn syrup

⇨ small saucepan with lid

⇨ stove

⇨ candy thermometer

⇨ electric mixer

⇨ measuring spoons

⇨ vanilla extract

⇨ spatula

⇨ 2 large airtight containers or 1-gallon (3.8 L) plastic bags

⇨ cutting board

⇨ pizza cutter

⇨ ruler

PART 1

1 Use masking tape and a pen or marker to label the outside of the cake or pie pans "1" and "2."

2 Pour a small amount of vegetable oil onto a paper towel. Lightly oil the insides of the cake or pie pans.

3 Pour a small amount of powdered sugar into the strainer. Lightly dust the pans with sugar. Set the pans aside.

4 Pour $\frac{1}{6}$ cup of water into the mixing bowl. Sprinkle 0.25 ounces (7 g) of gelatin over the water. Mix the gelatin and water with a fork for about 5 seconds. Set the mixing bowl aside.

5 Add ¼ cup of water, ½ cup of granulated sugar, and $\frac{1}{3}$ cup of corn syrup to the saucepan. Put the lid on the saucepan. Turn the stove on medium-high heat.

6 Check the solution in the saucepan every 30 seconds until it just comes to a boil. Remove the lid.

7 Use the candy thermometer to measure the temperature of the syrup mixture. Do not let the thermometer touch the bottom or sides of the pan. When the mixture reaches 240°F (116°C), turn off the stove.

8 Carefully pour the syrup mixture into the mixing bowl with the gelatin. Set the timer for 11 minutes. Turn the mixer on low speed.

9 Gradually increase the speed of the mixer until it is operating on high speed. Within 11 minutes, the mixture should become very thick and glossy. Add ½ teaspoon of vanilla. Beat for 1 minute.

10 Coat a spatula with vegetable oil. Use it to scoop the marshmallow mixture into pan 1. Smooth the mixture into the pan. Let it sit until the mixture is firm.

11 Repeat steps 4 to 10, this time using ¾ cup sugar and ⅙ cup corn syrup. Scoop this mixture into pan 2.

PART 2

1 Use masking tape and a pen or marker to label the airtight containers or plastic bags "1" and "2."

2 Once firm, turn the marshmallows from pan 1 onto a cutting board. Use the pizza cutter and ruler to cut the marshmallows into 1-inch (2.5 cm) squares. Dust the marshmallows with powdered sugar. Store the marshmallows in container 1 for up to a week.

3 Repeat step 2 with the marshmallows from pan 2.

4 Test your marshmallows! Drop a marshmallow from each batch into hot water. Which melts fastest? Repeat the test 3 times, and record your results.

5 Taste a marshmallow from each batch. Which is chewier? Which is softer? Which tastes better?

SCIENCE TAKEAWAY

The more sugar in a solution, the higher its boiling point. Batch 1 had a lower boiling point than batch 2. Batch 1 probably also melted faster, were softer, and were less sweet than batch 2. The amount of sugar in candy determines its structure. The more sugar, the harder the candy will be.

SUGAR GLASS

Have you ever watched a window shatter into a million pieces in a movie or TV show? Can you believe that window probably was made out of candy instead of real glass? Find out how to make your own sugar glass window.

🕐 **TIMEFRAME: 30 minutes**

MATERIALS

⇨ measuring spoons

⇨ measuring cups

⇨ cream of tartar

⇨ water

⇨ granulated sugar

⇨ light corn syrup

⇨ saucepan

⇨ candy thermometer

⇨ mixing bowl

⇨ ice cubes

⇨ aluminum baking pan

⇨ nonstick cooking spray or parchment paper

⇨ paper and pencil

⇨ stove

⇨ wooden spoon

⇨ timer or stopwatch

⇨ food coloring

⇨ metal fork

1 Combine 1/8 teaspoon of cream of tartar, 1 cup of water, 1¾ cups of sugar, and ½ cup of corn syrup in the saucepan. Place the candy thermometer in the saucepan, making sure it doesn't touch the bottom or sides.

2 Fill the mixing bowl half full of cold water. Add a few ice cubes.

3 Spray the baking pan with cooking spray or cover with parchment paper.

4 Create a table on your paper with 5 columns and 8 rows. Label the columns Temperature, Time, Appearance, Feel, and Other observations. Label the rows Room temperature 1, 230°F (110°C), 235°F (112°C), 245°F (118°C), 255°F (123°C), 275°F (135°C), 300°F (149°C), and Room temperature 2.

5 Look at the contents of the saucepan, and fill out row 1 of your table. Leave the Time column blank for now.

6 Place the saucepan on the stove on medium heat. Write down the time you began heating the pan in the Time column of row 1 on your table. Use the wooden spoon to stir the mixture until it comes to a slow boil.

7 When the thermometer reaches 230°F (110°C), use the wooden spoon to drop a small amount of the mixture into the bowl of ice water. Record the time in row 2 of your table.

8 When the sugar mixture cools, write your observations about it in row 2. How has the mixture changed since you began heating it?

9 Repeat steps 7 and 8 to fill out rows 3 to 7 of your table. When the mixture is between 300°F (149°C) and 310°F (154°C), carefully pour it into the baking pan. Smooth the mixture with a spoon.

10 Drop food coloring onto the surface of your mixture. Use a fork to swirl the colors.

11 After the mixture has cooled completely, remove your sugar glass from the pan. Record your observations in row 8 of your table. At what temperatures did you notice the biggest changes in the feel and appearance of the sugar mixture?

SCIENCE TAKEAWAY

Before you heated the sugar mixture, the solution was saturated. As you heated the mixture, the long sugar molecules broke into smaller pieces and dissolved into the water. As the solution boiled, the water evaporated, leaving higher concentrations of sugar. The more sugar, the harder the cooled mixture.

STILL HUNGRY?

Make sure to clean up the kitchen after every project. Wash your dishes, put away extra ingredients, and throw away or dump out any results you don't want to eat or drink.

What did you learn about the science of food? What would you still like to find out? You can try making your own changes to these projects to learn even more. Do any other candies dance in soda? Do people of different ages taste things differently? Can you think of a way to make your soda recipe even more delicious? Try it out!

For even more edible science projects, scan this QR code!

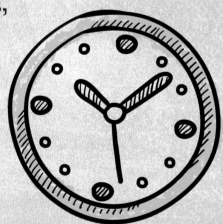

GLOSSARY

boiling point: the temperature at which a liquid boils

concentration: the amount of something in one place

dissolve: to become part of a liquid

distilled: made pure by removing all particles and minerals

evaporate: to change from liquid into gas

gas: a substance such as oxygen that has no fixed shape. Gas molecules have lots of space between them and fill the space they are in.

globule: a small, round mass

liquid: a substance such as water that flows freely. Liquid molecules are loosely connected and move around one another.

molecule: the smallest piece a material can be divided into without changing how it behaves

saturated: being unable to absorb or dissolve any more of something

solid: something that keeps its size and shape. Molecules in solids are tightly packed together.

solution: a mixture made up of a substance that has been dissolved in a liquid

FURTHER INFORMATION

For more information and projects, visit **Science Buddies** at **https://www.sciencebuddies.org/**.

Exploring Kitchen Science: 30+ Edible Experiments and Kitchen Science Activities. San Francisco: Weldon Owen, 2015.

Schloss, Andrew. *Amazing (Mostly) Edible Science: A Family Guide to Fun Experiments in the Kitchen.* Beverly, MA: Quarry, 2016.

Wheeler-Toppen, Jodi. *Edible Science: Experiments You Can Eat.* Washington, DC: National Geographic Society, 2015.

INDEX

PHOTO ACKNOWLEDGMENTS

The images in this book are used with the permission of: Design element (pencil) © primiaou/Shutterstock Images, pp. 8, 10, 12, 14, 16, 18, 20, 25, 29; © Visual Generation/Shutterstock Images, pp. 1 (clock), 30 (clock); © Mighty Media, Inc., pp. 1 (hot chocolate marshmallows), 3 (candy hearts, cups), 7 (plastic cup, serrated knife, ruler, hand mixer), 8–29 (project photos), 9 (worms), 12 (candy hearts), 13 (candy hearts), 16 (tongue), 18 (cups), 22 (hot chocolate marshmallows); © yoyoyai/Shutterstock Images, pp. 1 (ice cream, chocolate bar), 8 (chocolate bar), 20 (ice cream); © VectorShow/Shutterstock Images, pp. 1 (soda bottle), 14 (soda bottle); © asife/Shutterstock Images, p. 4 (boy drinking soda); © Christine Glade/Shutterstock Images, p. 5 (girls eating ice cream); © paulaphoto/Shutterstock Images, p. 6 (girl eating); © MARGRIT HIRSCH/Shutterstock Images, p. 7 (pot); © Tei Sinthip/Shutterstock Images, p. 7 (measuring spoons); © plantic/Shutterstock Images, p. 7 (boy opening oven); © Minur/Shutterstock Images, pp. 10 (butter), 11 (cream); © dicogm/Shutterstock Images, p. 24 (broken glass); © Tiwat K/Shutterstock Images, p. 31 (computer)

Front cover: © Squirrell/Shutterstock Images (pot); © STILLFX/Shutterstock Images (background); © Tiwat K/Shutterstock Images (apple); © Tom and Kwikki/Shutterstock Images (molecules); © Visual Generation/Shutterstock Images (clock); © yoyoyai/Shutterstock Images (ice cream cone)

Back cover: © primiaou/Shutterstock Images (light bulb, pencil); © Squirrell/Shutterstock Images (hand mixer); © STILLFX/Shutterstock Images (background); © Tom and Kwikki/Shutterstock Images (molecules); © VectorShow/Shutterstock Images (water bottle)